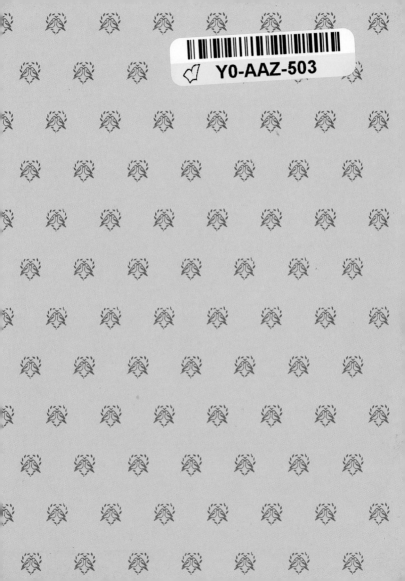

♈ L O V E S I G N S ♈

ARIES

March 21 – April 20

JULIA *&* DEREK PARKER

FIREFLY BOOKS

Dedicated to Martin Lethbridge

A DORLING KINDERSLEY BOOK

Project Editor • Annabel Morgan
Art Editor • Anna Benjamin
Managing Editor • Francis Ritter
Managing Art Editor • Derek Coombes
DTP Designer • Cressida Joyce
Production Controller • Martin Croshaw
US Editor • Constance M. Robinson

ACKNOWLEDGMENTS

Photography: Steve Gorton: pp. 10, 13–15, 17–19, 46–49; Ian O'Leary: 16. *Additional photography by:* Colin Keates, Dave King, Monique Le Luhandre, David Murray, Tim Ridley, Clive Streeter, Harry Taylor, Matthew Ward. *Artworks:* Nici Demin: 34–45; Peter Lawman: *jacket*, 4, 12; Paul Redgrave: 24–33; Satwinder Sehmi: *glyphs*; Jane Thomson: *borders*; Rosemary Woods: 11. Peter Lawman's paintings are exhibited by the Portal Gallery Ltd, London.

Picture credits: Bridgeman Art Library/Hermitage, St. Petersburg: 51; Robert Harding Picture Library: 20l, 20c, 20r; Images Colour Library: 9; The National Gallery, London: 11; Tony Stone Images: 21t, 21b; The Victoria and Albert Museum, London: 5; Zefa: 21c.

First published in Canada in 1996 by
Firefly Books Ltd., 3680 Victoria Park Avenue, Willowdale, Ontario M2H 3K1

Canadian Cataloguing in Publication Data
Parker, Julia and Derek
Love Signs

ISBN 1-55209-059-0

1. Astrology. 2. Love – Miscellanea. 3. Sex – Miscellanea. I. Title.
BF1729.L6P37 1996   133.5'864677   C96–931074–9

Reproduced by Bright Arts, Hong Kong
Printed and bound by Imago, Hong Kong

CONTENTS

Astrology & You 8

Looking for a Lover 10

You & Your Lover 12

The Food of Love 16

Places to Love 20

Venus & Mars 22

Your Love Life 24

Your Sex Life 34

Tokens of Love 46

Your Permanent Relationship 50

Venus & Mars Tables 52

ASTROLOGY & YOU

THERE IS MUCH MORE TO ASTROLOGY THAN YOUR SUN SIGN.
A SIMPLE INVESTIGATION INTO THE POSITION OF THE OTHER
PLANETS AT THE MOMENT OF YOUR BIRTH WILL PROVIDE YOU
WITH FASCINATING INSIGHTS INTO YOUR PERSONALITY.

*Y*our birth sign, or Sun sign, is the sign of the zodiac that the Sun occupied at the moment of your birth. The majority of books on astrology concentrate only on explaining the relevance of the Sun signs. This is a simple form of astrology that can provide you with some interesting but rather general information about you and your personality. In this book, we take you a step further, and reveal how the planets Venus and Mars work in association with your Sun sign to influence your attitudes toward romance and sexuality.

In order to gain a detailed insight into your personality, a "natal" horoscope, or birth chart, is necessary. This details the position of all the planets in our solar system at the moment of your birth, not just the position of the Sun. Just as the Sun occupied one of the 12 zodiac signs when you were born, perhaps making you "a Geminian" or "a Sagittarian," so each of the other planets occupied a certain sign. Each planet governs a different area of your personality, and the planets Venus and Mars are responsible for your attitudes toward love and sex, respectively.

For example, if you are a Sun-sign Sagittarian, according to the attributes of the sign you should be a dynamic, freedom-loving character. However, if Venus occupied Libra when you were born, you may make a passive and clinging partner – qualities that are supposedly completely alien to Sagittarians.

A MAP OF THE CONSTELLATION

*The 16th-century astronomer Copernicus first made the
revolutionary suggestion that the planets orbit the Sun
rather than Earth. In this 17th-century constellation chart,
the Sun is shown at the center of the solar system.*

The tables on pages 52–61 of this book will enable you to discover the positions of Mars and Venus at the moment of your birth. Once you have read this information, turn to pages 22–45. On these pages we explain how the influences of Venus and Mars interact with the characteristics of your Sun sign. This information will provide you with many illuminating insights into your personality, and explains how the planets have formed your attitudes toward love and sex.

LOOKING FOR A LOVER

ASTROLOGY CAN PROVIDE YOU WITH VALUABLE INFORMATION
ON HOW TO INITIATE AND MAINTAIN RELATIONSHIPS. IT CAN
ALSO TELL YOU HOW COMPATIBLE YOU ARE WITH YOUR LOVER,
AND HOW SUCCESSFUL YOUR RELATIONSHIP IS LIKELY TO BE.

*P*eople frequently use astrology to lead into a relationship, and "What sign are you?" is often used as a conversation opener. Some people simply introduce the subject as an opening gambit, while others place great importance on this question and its answer.

Astrology can affect the way you think and behave when you are in love. It can also provide you with fascinating information about your lovers and your relationships. Astrology cannot tell you who to fall in love with or who to avoid, but it can offer you some very helpful advice.

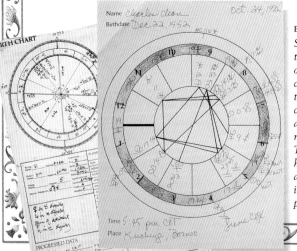

BIRTH CHARTS
Synastry involves the comparison of two people's charts in order to assess their compatibility in all areas of their relationship. The process can highlight any areas of common interest or potential conflict.

THE TABLE OF ELEMENTS
People whose signs are grouped under the same element tend to find it easy to fall into a happy relationship. The groupings are:
FIRE: *Aries, Leo, Sagittarius*
EARTH: *Taurus, Virgo, Capricorn*
AIR: *Gemini, Libra, Aquarius*
WATER: *Cancer, Scorpio, Pisces*

When you meet someone to whom you are attracted, astrology can provide you with a valuable insight into his or her personality. It may even reveal unattractive characteristics that your prospective partner is trying to conceal.

Astrologers are often asked to advise lovers involved in an ongoing relationship, or people who are contemplating a love affair. This important aspect of astrology is called synastry, and involves comparing the birth charts of the two people concerned. Each birth chart records the exact position of the planets at the moment and place of a person's birth.

By interpreting each chart separately, then comparing them, an astrologer can assess the compatibility of any two people, showing where problems may arise in their relationship, and where strong bonds will form.

One of the greatest astrological myths is that people of some signs are not compatible with people of certain other signs. This is completely untrue. Whatever your Sun sign, you can have a happy relationship with a person of any other sign.

YOU & YOUR LOVER

KNOWING ABOUT YOURSELF AND YOUR LOVER IS THE KEY TO
A HAPPY RELATIONSHIP. HERE WE REVEAL THE TRADITIONAL
ASSOCIATIONS OF ARIES, YOUR COMPATIBILITY WITH ALL THE
SUN SIGNS, AND THE FLOWERS LINKED WITH EACH SIGN.

HONEYSUCKLE
IS LINKED
TO ARIES

BRIGHT RED IS
TRADITIONALLY
ASSOCIATED
WITH ARIES

DIAMOND IS
THE ARIEN
GEMSTONE

THE PLANET
MARS RULES
ARIES

ARIENS ARE
USUALLY
SLIM AND
WIRY, WITH A
SPRINGY WALK

SHEEP AND RAMS
ARE CONSIDERED
TO BE ARIEN
ANIMALS

ARIES AND ARIES

When two fiery Ariens get together, sparks will fly. Your relationship will be fun-filled and affectionate, but it could also be stormy. You must both cultivate kindness and consideration.

Lavender is a Geminian flower

Thistles are ruled by Aries

ARIES AND GEMINI

A lively Geminian will keep you on your toes. Both of you are restless, and you share a love of novelty and excitement, but Geminian flirtatiousness may irritate you and cause quarrels.

ARIES AND TAURUS

A stolid Taurean will pant along behind an active Arien, and you may find their ponderousness a little irritating. However, once Taurean passions are aroused, you will have no complaints.

The lily, and other white flowers, are ruled by Cancer

The rose is associated with Taurus

ARIES AND CANCER

Cancerians long for emotional and domestic security, while you yearn for action, excitement, and adventure. However, Ariens will work hard to keep home-loving Cancerians comfortable.

ARIES AND LEO

The Arien motto is "me first," but fiery Leos also want to lead, and you may find yourselves battling for supremacy. However, you have much in common and can bring out the best in each other.

Hydrangeas are governed by Libra

Sunflowers are ruled by Leo

ARIES AND LIBRA

A classic attraction of opposites. Librans will cool your rather undignified Arien impetuousity and abrasiveness, while you will boost their energy levels. This should be a very happy union.

ARIES AND VIRGO

You are very different beings, and mutual interests must be cultivated. The Virgoan influence will bring you down to earth, and you will encourage your lover to take life a little less seriously.

Honeysuckle is attributed to Scorpio

ARIES AND SCORPIO

You are both very passionate. If your stormy emotions clash, unpleasant scenes will result. Ariens and Scorpios possess powerful libidos and are highly compatible sexually.

Small, brightly colored flowers are associated with Virgo

ARIES AND SAGITTARIUS

Sagittarians revel in the chase. The more eagerly you pursue them, the more pleasure they will take in evading your grasp. When you do get together, your alliance will be passionate.

Carnations are ruled by Sagittarius

ARIES AND CAPRICORN

Only the most motivated and ambitious Ariens will be suited to a calculating Capricorn. Your abundance of energy and enthusiasm should easily break down Capricorn coolness.

Pansies are Capricorn flowers

Orchids are associated with Aquarius

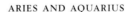

ARIES AND AQUARIUS

Aquarians make the best friends in the world and they will be attracted by your warmth and enthusiasm. You both value your independence highly, so this may have to be an open relationship.

Viburnum is governed by Pisces

ARIES AND PISCES

You are very different creatures. Pisceans are very dreamy and sentimental, with tears often close to the surface. However, their gentle romantic charms will soon win you over.

THE FOOD OF LOVE

WHEN PLANNING A SEDUCTION, THE SENSUOUS DELIGHTS OF AN
EXQUISITE MEAL SHOULD NEVER BE UNDERESTIMATED. READ ON
TO DISCOVER THE PERFECT MEAL FOR EACH OF THE SUN SIGNS,
GUARANTEED TO AROUSE INTEREST AND STIR DESIRE.

*Fiery Ariens
relish strongly
flavored and
exotic dishes,
such as spicy
mulligatawny soup.*

- THE FOOD OF LOVE -

FOR ARIENS
Spicy mulligatawny soup
·
Peppered steak
·
Baked Alaska

FOR TAUREANS
Cream of cauliflower soup
·
Tournedos Rossini
·
Rich chocolate and brandy mousse

FOR GEMINIANS
Seafood and avocado salad
·
Piquant stir-fried pork with ginger
·
Zabaglione

FOR CANCERIANS
Artichoke vinaigrette
·
Sole Bonne Femme
·
Almond soufflé

– THE FOOD OF LOVE –

FOR LEOS

Roasted tomato and garlic soup
·
Boeuf Stroganoff
·
Pears cooked in wine

FOR VIRGOS

Eggplant salad
·
Paella
·
French apple tart

FOR LIBRANS

Asparagus with hollandaise sauce
·
Pork with roasted apples
·
Strawberry Pavlova

FOR SCORPIOS

Vichyssoise
·
Lobster Newburg
·
Blueberry cream

- THE FOOD OF LOVE -

FOR SAGITTARIANS
Chilled cucumber soup
·
Nutty onion flan
·
Rhubarb crumble with fresh cream

FOR CAPRICORNS
Eggs Florentine
·
Pork tenderloin stuffed with sage
·
Pineapple Pavlova

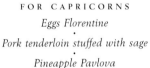

FOR AQUARIANS
Watercress soup
·
Chicken cooked with chili and lime
·
Lemon soufflé

FOR PISCEANS
French onion soup
·
Trout au vin rosé
·
Melon sorbet

PLACES TO LOVE

ONCE YOU HAVE WON YOUR LOVER'S HEART, A ROMANTIC
VACATION TOGETHER WILL SEAL YOUR LOVE. HERE, YOU
CAN DISCOVER THE PERFECT DESTINATION FOR EACH SUN
SIGN, FROM HISTORIC CITIES TO IDYLLIC BEACHES.

ARIES

*Florence is an Arien
city, and its perfectly
preserved Renaissance
palaces and churches
will set the scene for
wonderful romance.*

THE
EIFFEL
TOWER,
PARIS

TAURUS

*The unspoiled scenery
and unhurried pace
of life in rural Ireland
is sure to appeal to
patient and placid
Taureans.*

GEMINI

*Vivacious and restless
Geminians will feel at
home in the fast-paced
and sophisticated
atmosphere of
New York.*

CANCER

*The watery beauty
and uniquely romantic
atmosphere of Venice
is guaranteed to arouse
passion and stir the
Cancerian imagination.*

ST. BASIL'S
CATHEDRAL,
MOSCOW

AYERS ROCK/ULURU,
AUSTRALIA

THE PYRAMIDS,
EGYPT

LEO

*Leos will fall in love
all over again when
surrounded by the
picturesque charm and
unspoiled medieval
atmosphere of Prague.*

SAGITTARIUS

*The wide-ranging
spaces of the Australian
outback will appeal
to the Sagittarian love
of freedom and the
great outdoors.*

VIRGO

*Perhaps the most
elegant and romantic
of all cities, Paris is
certainly the ideal
setting for a stylish and
fastidious Virgo.*

CAPRICORN

*Capricorns will be
fascinated and inspired
by the great historical
monuments of Moscow,
the most powerful of all
Russian cities.*

GONDOLAS,
VENICE

LIBRA

*The dramatic and
exotic beauty of Upper
Egypt and the Nile will
provide the perfect
backdrop for wooing
a romantic Libran.*

AQUARIUS

*Intrepid Aquarians will
be enthralled and
amazed by the unusual
sights and spectacular
landscapes of the
Indian subcontinent.*

SCORPIO

*Intense and passionate
Scorpios will be strongly
attracted by the whiff
of danger present in
the exotic atmosphere
of New Orleans.*

PISCES

*Water-loving Pisceans
will be at their most
relaxed and romantic
by the sea, perhaps on
a small and unspoiled
Mediterranean island.*

THE TAJ MAHAL,
INDIA

VENUS & MARS

LUCID, SHINING VENUS AND FIERY, RED MARS HAVE ALWAYS
BEEN ASSOCIATED WITH HUMAN LOVE AND PASSION. THE TWO
PLANETS HAVE A POWERFUL INFLUENCE ON OUR ATTITUDES
TOWARD LOVE, SEX, AND RELATIONSHIPS.

*T*he study of astrology first began long before humankind began to record its own history. The earliest astrological artifacts discovered, scratches on bones recording the phases of the Moon, date from well before the invention of any alphabet or writing system.

The planets Venus and Mars have always been regarded as having enormous significance in astrology. This is evident from the tentative attempts of early astrologers to record the effects of the two planets on humankind. Hundreds of years later, the positions of the planets were carefully noted in personal horoscopes. The earliest known record is dated 410 BC: "Venus [was] in the Bull, and Mars in the Twins."

The bright, shining planet Venus represents the gentle effect of the soul on our physical lives. It is responsible for a refined and romantic sensuality – "pure" love, untainted by sex. Venus reigns over our attitudes toward romance and the spiritual dimension of love.

The planet Mars affects the physical aspects of our lives – our strength, both physical and mental; our endurance; and our ability to fight for survival. Mars is also strongly linked to the sex drive of both men and women. Mars governs our physical energy, sexuality, and levels of desire.

Venus is known as an "inferior" planet, because its orbit falls between Earth and the Sun. Venus orbits the Sun

LOVE CONQUERS ALL
In Botticelli's Venus and Mars, *the warlike, fiery
energy of Mars, the god of war, has been overcome by
the gentle charms of Venus, the goddess of love.*

closely, and its position in the
zodiac is always in a sign near
that of the Sun. As a result, the
planet can only have occupied
one of five given signs at the
time of your birth – your Sun
sign, or the two signs before or
after it. For example, if you were
born with the Sun in Virgo,
Venus can only have occupied
Cancer, Leo, Virgo, Libra, or
Scorpio at that moment.

Mars, on the other hand, is
a "superior" planet. Its orbit lies
on the other side of Earth from

the Sun, and therefore the
planet may have occupied any
of the 12 signs at the moment
of your birth.

On the following pages
(24–45) we provide you with
fascinating insights into how
Mars and Venus govern your
attitudes toward love, sex, and
relationships. To ascertain which
sign of the zodiac the planets
occupied at the moment of
your birth, you must first consult
the tables on pages 52–61. Then
turn to page 24 and read on.

YOUR LOVE LIFE

THE PLANET VENUS REPRESENTS LOVE, HARMONY, AND UNITY.
WORK OUT WHICH SIGN OF THE ZODIAC VENUS OCCUPIED AT
THE MOMENT OF YOUR BIRTH (SEE PAGES 52–57), AND READ ON.

VENUS IN AQUARIUS

From Aquarius, Venus sheds a glamorous light that will imbue you with an irresistible but slightly aloof aura.

Prospective partners will initially be intrigued by your elusive charm and friendly response. However, they may be surprised when, just as the atmosphere seems to be warming up, you pull away from them, becoming cold and remote.

This sudden coolness is due to the Aquarian influence. When Venus shines from Aquarius, the planet can bring with it a fear of emotional involvement. Although you will display all the typical passion and ardor of an Arien in love, you may feel apprehensive when your lover makes it clear that he or she

wants your relationship to enter into a more serious phase. Even if you feel ready to make a long-term commitment to your partner, you will still want to enjoy a sense of freedom and privacy within your relationship.

You scorn any pretense or deceit and dislike it in others. This devotion to honesty is most admirable, but it can make life rather difficult. When involved in a relationship, you will guard your solitude jealously, and will want to retain your independence. Your honesty and openness can be devastating, and you will tell your lover when you find someone else attractive. This candor may lead to painful confrontations with partners who have a jealous disposition.

If your relationship is to succeed, your partner must understand that you need to retain a sense of freedom and solitude. Your independence may be taken as a sign that you care only about yourself. Therefore, you should make an effort to be reassuring and convincing in your declarations of love. Your open and candid personality will prove invaluable in such situations, as you will only be able to allay your partner's fears through honest discussion and explanation of your feelings.

Ariens can be selfish, and it could be said that the Arien motto is "me first." Try to curb this aspect of your personality and encourage your generous and romantic side, which delights in giving unexpected presents, organizing unusual diversions, and lavishing attentions on your lover.

VENUS IN PISCES

*T*he combination of Venus in Pisces and the Sun in Aries is an entirely beneficial one. This placing of Venus softens the exuberant and hot-headed characteristics of Aries, and allows the gentler qualities of a water sign to cool down the heated passions of a fire sign.

From Pisces, Venus brings with her seductive elements of understanding and sympathy, which are not typical of the Arien character. With this planetary placement, you will be more ready to compromise and less assertive and impatient than many Ariens.

The influence of Venus in Pisces will not detract from the Arien capacity for sexual passion. Instead, the planet will add an element of the poetic and romantic to your personality, rendering you even more irresistible to potential partners.

You will be an adventurous yet sensitive lover, always considerate of your partner's feelings and happiness.

You are a true romantic, and will carefully set the scene for romance. Some Ariens may be content with the back seat of a car, but an elegant and comfortable seduction is more your style. In fact, you may be so concerned with comfort and luxury that money will seem no object, and you will need to curb your extravagance if the health of your bank balance is not to suffer unduly.

Ariens can fall in love with alarming speed. However, Ariens with Venus in Pisces are less impetuous, and will pause for thought before committing themselves. You tend to be more temperate and less dramatic than other Ariens, and will consider a situation from all angles, rather than throwing yourself at any potential lover.

Your Arien enthusiam will give you the ability to inspire and motivate your lover. You will eagerly encourage your partner to embark on new projects and to set ambitious goals in all areas of life. This valuable ability to boost your lover's confidence and be completely encouraging is a very attractive attribute, and one of the most important ingredients for a truly happy and successful relationship.

With an Arien, selfishness and self-indulgence are never very far beneath the surface. However, these unattractive qualities should be kept in firmly in check by the generosity and kindness of Pisces. When the passion of Aries and the intuitive sensitivity of Venus in Pisces combine, they will create a personality that is difficult to resist, and will make you a caring, passionate, and sensual lover.

VENUS IN ARIES

*A*n Arien with Venus in Aries is an Arien through and through. You will display all the characteristics typical of the sign when you are in love. You are enthusiastic, exuberant, and extravagant, and will spare no expense in catering to your lover's tastes. You want whoever you are with to have as good a time as you do. However, there is a danger that that this pampering will be so pleasing that your lover will simply lie back and luxuriate in your attentions rather than responding to you in kind.

Ariens can fall in love with all the immediacy of a bolt of lightning. Due to your double Arien influence, this is particularly likely to be true of you. Although your spontaneity and passion can be appealing, you tend to fall head over heels a little too easily, and can believe that you are passionately and deeply in love after the briefest encounter. Anything can bewitch you – a casual smile, the turn of a head, or even the clichéd meeting of eyes across a crowded room. Unfortunately, once you have gotten to know the object of your affections, it may become obvious that you are not well suited and the match is less than perfect.

Your Arien hotheadedness and impetuousity can take over. When you meet someone you are attracted to, try to keep your forcefulness in check. Some people are more cautious and timid than you, and may feel overwhelmed by your attentions. If you are intent on achieving a successful and long-lasting relationship, you must adopt a more rational approach. Try to take things slowly – this will reassure your lover and will prevent you from making any rash promises that you may

later regret. You must also resist the temptation to rush into a sexual relationship before your prospective partner feels ready to take such a step.

The typical Arien is not averse to the excitement and adventure of a quick fling. You may enjoy the thought of a swift seduction, followed by a hasty retreat in order to escape any unpleasant consequences or painful recriminations.

Try not to cause too much heartache to those who love you. Search your heart for the kinder and softer attributes of Venus, and consider the feelings of others. Be aware of the Arien tendency toward selfishness, which must be kept under control. You can combat this quality by asking yourself if you are putting yourself and your own interests and concerns before those of your partner.

VENUS IN TAURUS

*A*strologically, Venus is said to "rule" Taurus; therefore, the influence of Venus is particularly strong when the planet occupies this sign.

When Venus shines from Taurus, you will exercise real charm in every area of a relationship, and will display a strong capacity for straight-forward, honest affection. Taurean tenderness will soften the passion with which Ariens express themselves when in love. However, this does not mean that Arien passion will be inhibited by Venus in Taurus – if anything, it will be heightened by the position of the planet.

Due to the influence of Venus, you will be much more cautious than many Ariens, and you will not rush into an affair at a moment's notice. Therefore, you are less likely to make a dreadful mistake by heading straight for someone who

you find attractive, but who is disastrously unsuitable. Enthusiasm and prudence will combine to make you careful and discriminating in your choice of a lover, and you will choose both wisely and well.

You delight in giving pleasure, and will be very happy if your lover shares your interest in good food and entertainment. You are a good listener. Your friends and lovers, who will desire much of your attention, will become spoiled if you give into their demands too often.

From Taurus, Venus may bring you an unwelcome injection of possessiveness. Ariens are naturally somewhat selfish, and the quality of possessiveness can easily spring from that trait. Remember that no one likes to think of themselves as belonging to another person completely. If you do become jealous and

possessive, a damaging and claustrophobic atmosphere may pervade your relationship. To add insult to injury, you may demand a measure of freedom for yourself while trying to lock your lover away from others. The best way to deal with these problems is to accept that they may occur, and to keep a sharp eye out for any negative emotions so you can release them as soon as they appear.

Taureans revel in luxury, and love pampering themselves. Some of this sensual enjoyment will be communicated to you when Venus is in Taurus. You will revel in the material comforts and pleasures of life, and will want to share them with your partner.

Sensual contact with your lover will play an important role in your relationship, and you are likely to be a deliberate, leisurely, and exciting lover.

VENUS IN GEMINI

*L*ight-hearted Geminian affection will lighten the intensity of Arien passion. You delight in friendship and fun within a partnership, and will find these aspects of your relationship just as rewarding as sexual pleasure.

Common pursuits and mutual interests are very important to you. You will thrive upon a healthy sense of competition within your relationship, and will expect your partner to provide you with plenty of challenges, both intellectual and physical.

However, despite your lively charm and beguiling vivacity, there are potential dangers in this planetary combination. Gemini is notoriously flirtatious and restless and could tempt you to become involved in a number of affairs at the same time. You may find yourself getting into serious trouble simply because you cannot resist the thrill of becoming involved with more than one person at a time.

Ariens can be selfish and self-indulgent, and it is likely that you will constantly have to fight the temptation to be unfaithful. Your attitude toward love is playful and high-spirited, and you may find it hard to understand why others adopt such a serious and solemn approach. If your infidelity is discovered, you will use all your subtle charm to try and wriggle out of trouble. This may work once or twice, but in the end you will simply have to admit your sins. Talking things through with your lover might help, and as Mercury rules Gemini, you should be a good communicator. Unless you have an unusually understanding partner, you will have to subdue your tendency to play the field if your relationship is to survive.

Although you display all the usual elements of Arien passion, Gemini may make you slightly less emotional and sensitive. As a result, you may regard a quick fling as an insignificant episode, finding it difficult to understand or sympathize if your partner of the night, week, or month becomes emotionally involved, or even falls in love with you. You may not realize how callous your attitude is, or how much heartache you may cause, until you yourself become emotionally involved and suffer the pains of rejection.

Those born with Venus in Gemini will be attracted to lively, vivacious people who are outgoing and sociable. Physical beauty will not be of great importance to you – it will be a good sense of humor, a cheerful manner, and a curious mind that will win you over.

YOUR SEX LIFE

THE PLANET MARS REPRESENTS PHYSICAL AND SEXUAL ENERGY.
WORK OUT WHICH SIGN OF THE ZODIAC MARS OCCUPIED AT THE
MOMENT OF YOUR BIRTH (SEE PAGES 58–61), AND READ ON.

MARS IN ARIES

The energy and passion of Mars will exacerbate your exuberant Arien sexuality, and the result could be explosive.

Your high levels of sexual desire will fill you with energy, and if you cannot find an outlet for this abundance of energy, you may become frustrated and dissatisfied. You will be a dynamic and passionate lover, but the typical Arien tendency to be selfish may be increased by this placing, and therefore you should remember to consider your partner's sexual needs as well as your own.

Despite a somewhat unpredictable temper, you will be a warm and supportive lover.

MARS IN TAURUS

*F*rom Taurus, Mars will reinforce your abundant sex drive, and add sensuality and affection to your personality. However, it may also give you a somewhat possessive attitude toward your partner.

A helping of Taurean patience will make you less tempestuous than many Ariens, but once your adrenaline is flowing, you will make your feelings abundantly clear. Outbursts of temper can relieve your feelings but may also damage your relationship.

The combination of Taurean determination and Arien physical vigor will enable you to complete tasks thoroughly and swiftly, and you will be very adept around the house. However, the same tenacity and perseverance may combine to make you very stubborn in love.

The Taurean love of routine could have a negative effect on your sex life. Variety is the spice of life, so surprise your partner from time to time, and keep boredom firmly at bay.

MARS IN GEMINI

*D*ue to the influence of Mars in Gemini, you will fall in love even more quickly and passionately than your fellow Ariens. You have a lively and assertive manner, and will woo your potential lovers with charm and wit.

Mars is in a restless mood when it occupies Gemini. Once you have become involved in a relationship, you will expect it to develop quickly. When it is established, you will be eager to keep it lively and challenging, with a varied and exciting sex life. As soon as you cease to feel stimulated by your relationship, there is a danger that you will turn to infidelity to provide you with a forbidden thrill.

You may even experience a strong temptation to become involved in two or more affairs at the same time, which will bring additional complications. Arien sexuality is very strong, and will not be lessened by Mars shining from a relatively cool sign such as Gemini.

MARS IN CANCER

When Mars shines from Cancer, there is a strong emphasis on emotional passion. You will be a sensual and caring lover, very conscious of your partner's desires and eager to satisfy them. However, do not become too protective, or you may create a claustrophobic and confining atmosphere.

Due to the Cancerian influence, you are likely to have a need for emotional security. You will require frequent sexual contact, perhaps to be reassured that you are loved and desired. Your home will be your refuge, and from Cancer, Mars will give you a strong homemaking instinct. Incidentally, when the planet occupies this sign, it is said to increase fertility.

The combination of Arien emotion and Cancerian over-sensitivity can lead to explosions. In moments of anger you can be cruel, and may make scathing comments with the intention of hurting others. Try to hold your tongue during such encounters.

MARS IN LEO

*W*hen Mars shines from Leo, your boundless Arien energy will be heightened, making you an enthusiastic and vivacious companion.

You enjoy being in love, and will want your partner to share in this enjoyment. Sex is one of your greatest pleasures, and your lovemaking is passionate and lavish. You revel in luxury, and your lover will be seduced with fine food and drink, and pampered in the most luxurious surroundings that you can afford.

You may find yourself – quite unintentionally – adopting the dominant position within your relationship, especially if your lover is less extroverted than you. Try to subdue your leonine tendency to take over, otherwise you could appear autocratic and domineering.

Although you may have a hot temper, you never bear a grudge, and you detest small-mindedness and pettiness. Angry words will be quickly forgiven, and arguments swiftly forgotten.

MARS IN VIRGO

*F*rom Virgo, Mars can bring a high level of nervous energy. You may find it hard to relax, and might feel that you should always be busy and industrious. This does not create a tranquil or relaxed atmosphere in which to cultivate a friendship or develop a relationship.

You are likely to possess a powerful Arien sex drive, but may find it difficult to express your desires openly. This is because the Virgoan influence from Mars can be inhibiting, and

you may find that the natural nervousness that accompanies the early stages of a new relationship is so strong that it leads to nervous tension. Try to relax and follow your valuable natural instincts, rather than attempting to repress them.

Virgo is a very discriminating sign, and Mars will bring you some of this quality. Do not let your keen critical faculty obstruct your enthusiastic Arien sexuality, and try not to be over-critical of your partners.

MARS IN LIBRA

The fiery dynamism of Mars is weakened when it occupies Libra, and as a result you may be reluctant to draw on your potent stores of Arien energy. You can be rather languid in your approach to sex, and you may even find yourself thinking up excuses to avoid sexual activity. Remember, there is a limit to the number of headaches you can feign in a week.

However, once you are aroused, your partner will have no complaints, for your sexuality is actually heightened by this placing of Mars. When you are in the right mood, you are a passionate and enthusiastic lover. Your poetic sense of romance and your charming idealistic streak are particularly attractive attributes.

Do not allow the softening effect of Mars in Libra to weaken your powerful Arien sexuality. Instead, use the gentle influence of the sign to lessen any Arien abrasiveness and tame your fiery temper.

MARS IN SCORPIO

*M*ars in Scorpio is a powerful combination, and can be explosive. When Scorpio energy is communicated by fiery Mars to a spirited Arien personality, sparks can fly.

There is wonderful potential in this dynamic combination. Provided that your emotions are expressed positively, your lover will have no cause for complaint. Jealousy may present a slight problem, and you may have to combat this destructive emotion with self-knowledge. Admit to yourself that you can be unreasonably and irrationally jealous. You need to recognize your failing and develop a way to cope with it.

From Scorpio, Mars increases the sexual vigor of Aries, and this energy must find a satisfying outlet. Sexual frustration could lead to resentfulness, irritability, and a brooding unhappiness.

The genitals are the part of the body governed by Scorpio; problems in that area should be attended to immediately.

MARS IN SAGITTARIUS

*T*his combination gives an enormous boost to your physical energy. If this energy is not positively channeled, it can lead to a sense of restlessness as well as a constant search for novelty and excitement.

The influence of Sagittarius may bring you a high libido and a wandering eye, which could lead to illicit affairs and intrigues. If your sexual needs are not satisfied within your relationship, there is a danger that you may turn to infidelity and deceit.

Sagittarians have a very low boredom threshold. You need plenty of variety in your sex life. Predictable, unexciting sex will give your relationship the kiss of death. Imaginative, experimental sex is what you enjoy, and you are a completely uninhibited lover.

You are a demonstrative and affectionate partner with a cheerful manner. A lover who can stimulate your mind and has a considerable sexual appetite will be your perfect match.

MARS IN CAPRICORN

*W*hen Mars shines from Capricorn, its influence will make you determined and energetic. These qualities will combine with your Arien competitiveness and will to win. When you fall in love, you will be determined to carry off what you see as the first prize.

Although you appear cool and controlled, you have a strong sex drive and enjoy physical contact. You value your dignity highly, and your air of calm detachment is largely due to your fear of rejection. However, once involved in a long-term relationship, you make an ardent and sensual lover.

After the initial courtship, your lover may find that reality does not live up to expectations. To win your partner's affections, you will have initially bestowed a considerable amount of attention. If you are successful, the primary importance of your career may assert itself. If this is not controlled, you may lose your lover altogether.

MARS IN AQUARIUS

*W*hen Mars is placed in Aquarius, it will take the edge off your emotional and physical expression of love and will cool your ardor, giving you a more balanced and fulfilling love life. This is a great benefit, because Arien relationships can assume rather a hectic pace.

When you first become romantically involved, you may perceive that your prospective partner is more eager than you are to make a commitment. Due to the Aquarian influence

from Mars, you need your freedom, and you may not share your lover's eagerness to enter into a long-term commitment.

You enjoy sex and will be eager to experiment, although the Aquarian influence may slightly restrain your Arien physical passion. Mars will also lessen your Arien selfishness. You will be more interested in satisfying your lover's desire, and less preoccupied with your own enjoyment – a truly beneficial development.

MARS IN PISCES

*M*ars in Pisces creates a sensual, passionate, and considerate lover, and will raise your emotions to a high level. Since Ariens tend to be very passionate and highly sexual, no lover of yours is ever likely to have to complain of any physical or emotional neglect.

Problems may arise if your abundance of sexual and emotional energy is not positively channeled. Physical exercise and an active sex life should help to work off any excess energy.

If any obstacles are allowed to block the flow of your sexual energy, a sense of restlessness and frustration may result.

You are an ardent and expert lover with a truly erotic approach, and sex will play a central role in your relationship. However, a wonderful sex life is not enough to sustain a relationship, and unless you are genuinely happy with your lover when involved in mundane day-to-day tasks, there may be potential problems on the horizon.

TOKENS OF LOVE

ASTROLOGY CAN GIVE YOU A FASCINATING INSIGHT INTO
YOUR LOVER'S PERSONALITY AND ATTITUDE TOWARD LOVE. IT
CAN ALSO PROVIDE YOU WITH SOME INVALUABLE HINTS WHEN
YOU WANT TO CHOOSE A PERFECT GIFT FOR YOUR LOVER.

INDIAN HAIR
ORNAMENT

DRAMATICALLY
PATTERNED
SILK
SCARF

ARIES

*Ariens love brightly colored
clothes and accessories such as
patterned scarves or woolly
sweaters. The head is the body
part ruled by Aries, and unusual
hair accessories will
be appreciated.*

LIMOGES
PORCELAIN
PILLBOX

TAURUS

*Taureans value
quality above quantity.
They will adore fine
hand-painted porcelain,
or exquisite chocolates.*

BOX OF BELGIAN
CHOCOLATES

JORDAN
ALMONDS

GEMINI

*A handsome box of Jordan almonds
or mixed nuts is guaranteed to
please your Geminian lover.*

HEART-
SHAPED
SOAP

CANCER

*Cancerians will be delighted
by luxurious soap, and will
cherish anything decorated
with pearl, which is
their birthstone.*

PEARL
NECKLACE

KILIM
CUSHION

ANTIQUE
INDIAN
PERFUME
BOTTLE

LEO

*A dramatically colored
embroidered cushion, an
original painting, or a bottle
of expensive perfume will
all thrill your Leo lover.*

CARVED
AFRICAN
SPOON

CRYSTALLIZED
FRUITS

VIRGO

*Any objects made from wood will
delight Virgos because they are
drawn to natural materials. They
will enjoy a box of crystallized
fruit far more than chocolates.*

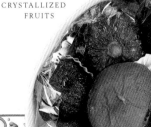

– TOKENS OF LOVE –

LIBRA
*Board or card games will
amuse your Libran lover.
They are true romantics,
and will also appreciate
a video of a
classic film.*

POSTER FOR
CLASSIC FILM

1930s
GAME
BOARD

SCENTED
BATH OIL

PATTERNED
TOOTHBRUSH

HAND-
PAINTED
GLOBE
PILLBOX

SCORPIO
*Scorpio is a water
sign; therefore,
unusual bathroom
accessories and
bath products are
always welcome.
Leather goods, such
as an attractive
belt or wallet,
will also please
a Scorpio lover.*

SAGITTARIUS
*Adventurous
Sagittarians love
to travel; therefore,
travel books and
accessories, such as
antique maps or
compasses, will be
greatly treasured.*

HEART-PATTERNED CANDLES

IVY

BUTTERFLY BROOCH

CAPRICORN

Elegant candles or an antique silver picture frame are the perfect gift for your Capricorn lover. If you want to give your lover a plant, choose ivy.

AQUARIUS

Glittering pieces of costume jewelry will charm an Aquarian, as will handmade modern pottery.

POTTERY MUG

PEARLY TURBAN SHELL

ITALIAN CLOWN MASK

PISCES

A decorative mask will appeal to a Piscean's shy, secretive side. Pisces is a water sign, and a pretty shell will delight Pisceans.

GIVING A BIRTHSTONE

DIAMOND

The most personal gift you can give your lover is the gem linked to his or her Sun sign.

ARIES: *diamond*
TAURUS: *emerald*
GEMINI: *agate* • CANCER: *pearl*
LEO: *ruby* • VIRGO: *sardonyx*
LIBRA: *sapphire* • SCORPIO: *opal*
SAGITTARIUS: *topaz*
CAPRICORN: *amethyst*
AQUARIUS: *aquamarine*
PISCES: *moonstone*

YOUR PERMANENT
RELATIONSHIP

EXUBERANT, AMBITIOUS ARIENS MAKE GENEROUS AND
ENTHUSIASTIC LOVERS, BUT FIRST THEY MUST OVERCOME
THE TYPICAL ARIEN PROPENSITY TOWARDS SELFISHNESS.

*T*he natural exuberance and enthusiastic approach to sexuality so typical of this sign makes you an excellent long-term partner. Your Arien optimism and enthusiasm are particularly attractive traits.

Ariens sometimes experience a great urge for change in their life. As a result they may rush into a relationship without giving it enough thought. You can fall in love with an alarming swiftness, and, when infatuated, will comply with any conditions in your eagerness to win the object of your affections. As a result, any fundamental incompatibilities may reveal themselves only later in your relationship, when you discover more about each other.

Ariens tend to be ambitious and competitive, and you will strive to be top of the class, the winner of the race, or the chairperson of the board. Ambition is a positive attribute, but do not devote so much time to your work and hobbies that you deprive your partner of your company. Your career and other interests should not endanger your domestic life by taking up an excessive amount of time.

The worst Arien fault is selfishness. This unattractive quality can manifest itself in a number of ways, and can cause problems within a relationship. It may not always be easy for you to recognize when you are acting in a selfish and inconsiderate fashion, or to understand your

A JOINT FUTURE
On a Sailing Ship, *by Caspar David Friedrich, shows a newly married couple sailing into a bright but unknown future together.*

partner's point of view when he or she objects to your self-centered behavior.

Try to cultivate mutual interests, which will help you remain content and satisfied with your partner. Common interests will encourage you to spend more time together, reducing the likelihood of you seeking emotional fulfillment elsewhere.

You must strive to achieve equilibrium in every sphere of your life. Balance the time that you devote to your own pursuits with time spent with your partner. Sometimes you will have to forget your own ambitions and preoccupations, and instead focus on supporting your partner. If you can achieve a sense of balance and show consideration for your partner, you will make a loving and generous companion.

VENUS & MARS TABLES

THESE TABLES WILL ENABLE YOU TO DISCOVER WHICH SIGNS
VENUS AND MARS OCCUPIED AT THE MOMENT OF YOUR BIRTH.
TURN TO PAGES 24–45 TO INVESTIGATE THE QUALITIES OF THESE
SIGNS, AND TO FIND OUT HOW THEY WORK WITH YOUR SUN SIGN.

*T*he tables on pages 53–61 will enable you to discover the positions of Venus and Mars at the moment of your birth.

First find your year of birth on the top line of the appropriate table, then find your month of birth in the left-hand column. Where the column for your year of birth intersects with the row for your month of birth, you will find a group of figures and zodiacal glyphs. These figures and glyphs show which sign of the zodiac the planet occupied

on the first day of that month, and any date during that month on which the planet moved into another sign.

For example, to ascertain the position of Venus on May 10, 1968, run your finger down the column marked 1968 until you reach the row for May. The row of numbers and glyphs shows that Venus occupied Aries on May 1, entered Taurus on May 4, and then moved into Gemini on May 28. Therefore, on May 10, Venus was in Taurus.

If you were born on a day when one of the planets was moving into a new sign, it may be impossible to determine your Venus and Mars signs completely accurately. If the characteristics described on the relevant pages do not seem to apply to you, read the interpretation of the sign before and after. One of these signs will be appropriate.

ZODIACAL GLYPHS

♈	Aries	♎	Libra
♉	Taurus	♏	Scorpio
♊	Gemini	♐	Sagittarius
♋	Cancer	♑	Capricorn
♌	Leo	♒	Aquarius
♍	Virgo	♓	Pisces

♀	1921	1922	1923	1924	1925	1926	1927	1928
JAN	1 ♒ 7 ♓	1 ♑ 25 ♒	1 ♏ 3 ♐	1 ♒ 20 ♓	1 ♐ 15 ♑	1 ♒	1 ♑ 10 ♒	1 ♏ 5 ♐ 30 ♑
FEB	1 ♓ 3 ♈	1 ♒ 18 ♓	1 ♐ 7 ♑ 14 ♒	1 ♓ 14 ♈	1 ♑ 8 ♒	1 ♒	1 ♒ 3 ♓ 27 ♈	1 ♑ 23 ♒
MAR	1 ♈ 8 ♉	1 ♓ 14 ♈	1 ♑ 7 ♒	1 ♈ 10 ♉	1 ♒ 5 ♓ 29 ♈	1 ♒	1 ♈ 23 ♉	1 ♒ 19 ♓
APR	1 ♉ 26 ♈	1 ♈ 7 ♉	1 ♓ 2 ♈ 27 ♓	1 ♉ 6 ♊	1 ♈ 22 ♉	1 ♒ 7 ♓	1 ♉ 17 ♊	1 ♓ 12 ♈
MAY	1 ♈	1 ♉ 8 ♊	1 ♓ 22 ♈	1 ♊ 7 ♋	1 ♉ 16 ♊	1 ♓	1 ♊ 13 ♋	1 ♈ 7 ♉ 31 ♊
JUN	1 ♈ 3 ♉	1 ♋ 20 ♌	1 ♈ 16 ♉	1 ♋	1 ♊ 10 ♋	1 ♓ 3 ♈ 29 ♉	1 ♊ 8 ♋	1 ♊ 24 ♋
JUL	1 ♉ 9 ♊	1 ♌ 16 ♍	1 ♉ 11 ♊	1 ♋	1 ♋ 4 ♌ 29 ♍	1 ♉ 25 ♊	1 ♊	1 ♋ 19 ♌
AUG	1 ♊ 6 ♋	1 ♍ 11 ♎	1 ♊ 4 ♋ 28 ♌	1 ♋	1 ♍ 23 ♎	1 ♊ 18 ♋	1 ♊ 19 ♋	1 ♌ 12 ♍
SEP	1 ♌ 27 ♍	1 ♎ 8 ♏	1 ♌ 22 ♍	1 ♋ 8 ♌	1 ♎ 17 ♏	1 ♋ 12 ♌	1 ♌	1 ♍ 5 ♎ 30 ♏
OCT	1 ♍ 21 ♎	1 ♏ 11 ♐	1 ♍ 16 ♎	1 ♌ 11 ♍	1 ♏ 12 ♐	1 ♌ 6 ♍ 30 ♎	1 ♍	1 ♏ 24 ♐
NOV	1 ♎ 14 ♏	1 ♐ 29 ♑	1 ♎ 9 ♏	1 ♍ 9 ♎	1 ♐ 7 ♑	1 ♎ 23 ♏	1 ♍ 10 ♎	1 ♐ 18 ♑
DEC	1 ♏ 8 ♐	1 ♏	1 ♐ 3 ♑ 27 ♒	1 ♎ 6 ♏	1 ♑ 6 ♒	1 ♏ 17 ♐	1 ♎ 9 ♏	1 ♑ 13 ♒

♀	1929	1930	1931	1932	1933	1934	1935	1936
JAN	1 ♒ 7 ♓	1 ♑ 25 ♒	1 ♏ 4 ♐	1 ♒ 20 ♓	1 ♐ 15 ♑	1 ♒	1 ♑ 9 ♒	1 ♏ 4 ♐ 29 ♑
FEB	1 ♓ 3 ♈	1 ♒ 17 ♓	1 ♐ 7 ♑ 13 ♒	1 ♓ 13 ♈	1 ♑ 8 ♒	1 ♒	1 ♒ 2 ♓ 27 ♈	1 ♑ 23 ♒
MAR	1 ♈ 9 ♉	1 ♓ 13 ♈	1 ♑ 6 ♒	1 ♈ 9 ♉	1 ♒ 4 ♓ 28 ♈	1 ♒	1 ♈ 23 ♉	1 ♒ 18 ♓
APR	1 ♉ 21 ♈	1 ♈ 7 ♉	1 ♓ 6 ♈	1 ♉ 6 ♊	1 ♈ 21 ♉	1 ♒ 7 ♓	1 ♉ 17 ♊	1 ♓ 12 ♈
MAY	1 ♈	1 ♉ 26 ♊	1 ♓ 22 ♈	1 ♊ 7 ♋	1 ♉ 16 ♊	1 ♓	1 ♊ 12 ♋	1 ♈ 6 ♉ 30 ♊
JUN	1 ♈ 4 ♉	1 ♋ 20 ♌	1 ♈ 15 ♉	1 ♋	1 ♊ 9 ♋	1 ♓ 3 ♈ 29 ♉	1 ♊ 8 ♋	1 ♊ 24 ♋
JUL	1 ♉ 9 ♊	1 ♌ 15 ♍	1 ♉ 10 ♊	1 ♋	1 ♋ 4 ♌ 28 ♍	1 ♉ 24 ♊	1 ♊	1 ♋ 18 ♌
AUG	1 ♊ 6 ♋	1 ♍ 11 ♎	1 ♊ 4 ♋ 28 ♌	1 ♋	1 ♍ 22 ♎	1 ♊ 18 ♋	1 ♍	1 ♌ 12 ♍
SEP	1 ♌ 26 ♍	1 ♎ 8 ♏	1 ♌ 21 ♍	1 ♋ 9 ♌	1 ♍ 16 ♎	1 ♌ 12 ♍	1 ♌	1 ♌ 5 ♍ 29 ♎
OCT	1 ♍ 21 ♎	1 ♏ 11 ♐	1 ♍ 15 ♎	1 ♌ 8 ♍	1 ♏ 12 ♐	1 ♌ 6 ♍ 30 ♎	1 ♍	1 ♏ 24 ♐
NOV	1 ♎ 14 ♏	1 ♐ 23 ♏	1 ♍ 8 ♎	1 ♎ 3 ♏ 28 ♐	1 ♐ 7 ♑	1 ♎ 23 ♏	1 ♍ 10 ♎	1 ♐ 17 ♑
DEC	1 ♏ 8 ♐ 31 ♑	1 ♏	1 ♐ 2 ♑ 26 ♒	1 ♏ 6 ♐	1 ♑ 6 ♒	1 ♏ 17 ♐	1 ♎ 17 ♏	1 ♑ 12 ♒

♀ 1937–1944

♀	1937	1938	1939	1940	1941	1942	1943	1944
JAN	1 ♒ · 7 ♓	1 ♑ · 24 ♒	1 ♏ · 5 ♐	1 ♒ · 19 ♓	1 ♐ · 14 ♑	1 ♒	1 ♑ · 9 ♒	1 ♏ · 4 ♐ · 29 ♑
FEB	1 ♓ · 3 ♈	1 ♒ · 17 ♓	1 ♐ · 7 ♑	1 ♓ · 13 ♈	1 ♑ · 7 ♒	1 ♒	1 ♒ · 2 ♓ · 26 ♈	1 ♑ · 22 ♒
MAR	1 ♈ · 10 ♉	1 ♓ · 13 ♈	1 ♑ · 6 ♒	1 ♈ · 9 ♉	1 ♒ · 3 ♓ · 28 ♈	1 ♒	1 ♈ · 22 ♉	1 ♒ · 18 ♓
APR	1 ♉ · 15 ♈	1 ♈ · 6 ♉ · 30 ♊	1 ♓ · 26 ♈	1 ♉ · 5 ♊	1 ♈ · 21 ♉	1 ♒ · 7 ♓	1 ♉ · 16 ♊	1 ♓ · 11 ♈
MAY	1 ♈	1 ♊ · 25 ♋	1 ♈ · 21 ♉	1 ♊ · 7 ♋	1 ♉ · 15 ♊	1 ♓ · 7 ♈	1 ♊ · 12 ♋	1 ♈ · 5 ♉ · 30 ♊
JUN	1 ♈ · 5 ♉	1 ♋ · 19 ♌	1 ♉ · 8 ♊	1 ♋	1 ♊ · 8 ♋	1 ♈ · 3 ♉ · 28 ♊	1 ♋ · 8 ♌	1 ♊ · 23 ♋
JUL	1 ♉ · 8 ♊	1 ♌ · 15 ♍	1 ♊ · 10 ♋	1 ♋ · 6 ♊	1 ♋ · 3 ♌ · 28 ♍	1 ♊ · 24 ♋	1 ♌ · 8 ♍	1 ♋ · 18 ♌
AUG	1 ♊ · 5 ♋	1 ♍ · 10 ♎	1 ♋ · 3 ♌ · 27 ♍	1 ♊ · 2 ♋	1 ♍ · 22 ♎	1 ♋ · 18 ♌	1 ♍	1 ♌ · 11 ♍
SEP	1 ♌ · 26 ♍	1 ♎ · 8 ♏	1 ♍ · 21 ♎	1 ♋ · 9 ♌	1 ♎ · 16 ♏	1 ♌ · 11 ♍	1 ♍	1 ♍ · 4 ♎ · 29 ♏
OCT	1 ♍ · 20 ♎	1 ♏ · 14 ♐	1 ♎ · 15 ♏	1 ♌ · 7 ♍	1 ♏ · 11 ♐	1 ♍ · 5 ♎ · 29 ♏	1 ♍	1 ♏ · 23 ♐
NOV	1 ♎ · 13 ♏	1 ♐ · 16 ♏	1 ♏ · 8 ♐	1 ♍ · 2 ♎ · 27 ♏	1 ♐ · 7 ♑	1 ♏ · 22 ♐	1 ♍ · 10 ♎	1 ♐ · 17 ♑
DEC	1 ♏ · 7 ♐ · 31 ♑	1 ♏	1 ♐ · 2 ♑ · 26 ♒	1 ♏ · 21 ♐	1 ♑ · 6 ♒	1 ♐ · 16 ♑	1 ♎ · 9 ♏	1 ♑ · 12 ♒

♀ 1945–1952

♀	1945	1946	1947	1948	1949	1950	1951	1952
JAN	1 ♒ · 6 ♓	1 ♑ · 23 ♒	1 ♏ · 6 ♐	1 ♒ · 19 ♓	1 ♐ · 14 ♑	1 ♒	1 ♑ · 8 ♒	1 ♏ · 3 ♐ · 28 ♑
FEB	1 ♓ · 3 ♈	1 ♒ · 16 ♓	1 ♐ · 7 ♑	1 ♓ · 12 ♈	1 ♑ · 7 ♒	1 ♒	1 ♓ · 25 ♈	1 ♑ · 21 ♒
MAR	1 ♈ · 12 ♉	1 ♓ · 11 ♈	1 ♑ · 6 ♒	1 ♈ · 9 ♉	1 ♒ · 3 ♓ · 27 ♈	1 ♒	1 ♈ · 22 ♉	1 ♒ · 17 ♓
APR	1 ♉ · 8 ♈	1 ♈ · 6 ♉ · 30 ♊	1 ♓ · 26 ♈	1 ♉ · 5 ♊	1 ♈ · 20 ♉	1 ♒ · 7 ♓	1 ♉ · 16 ♊	1 ♓ · 10 ♈
MAY	1 ♈	1 ♊ · 25 ♋	1 ♈ · 21 ♉	1 ♊ · 8 ♋	1 ♉ · 15 ♊	1 ♓ · 6 ♈	1 ♊ · 12 ♋	1 ♈ · 5 ♉ · 29 ♊
JUN	1 ♈ · 5 ♉	1 ♋ · 19 ♌	1 ♉ · 14 ♊	1 ♋	1 ♊ · 8 ♋	1 ♈ · 2 ♉ · 28 ♊	1 ♋ · 8 ♌	1 ♊ · 23 ♋
JUL	1 ♉ · 8 ♊	1 ♌ · 14 ♍	1 ♊ · 9 ♋	1 ♋ · 3 ♊	1 ♋ · 2 ♌ · 27 ♍	1 ♊ · 23 ♋	1 ♌ · 9 ♍	1 ♋ · 17 ♌
AUG	1 ♊ · 5 ♋ · 31 ♌	1 ♍ · 10 ♎	1 ♋ · 3 ♌ · 27 ♍	1 ♊ · 4 ♋	1 ♍ · 21 ♎	1 ♋ · 17 ♌	1 ♍	1 ♌ · 10 ♍
SEP	1 ♌ · 25 ♍	1 ♎ · 8 ♏	1 ♍ · 20 ♎	1 ♋ · 9 ♌	1 ♎ · 15 ♏	1 ♌ · 11 ♍	1 ♍	1 ♍ · 4 ♎ · 28 ♏
OCT	1 ♍ · 19 ♎	1 ♏ · 17 ♐	1 ♎ · 14 ♏	1 ♌ · 7 ♍	1 ♏ · 11 ♐	1 ♍ · 5 ♎ · 29 ♏	1 ♍	1 ♏ · 23 ♐
NOV	1 ♎ · 13 ♏	1 ♐ · 9 ♏	1 ♏ · 7 ♐	1 ♍ · 2 ♎ · 27 ♏	1 ♐ · 7 ♑	1 ♏ · 22 ♐	1 ♍ · 10 ♎	1 ♐ · 16 ♑
DEC	1 ♏ · 7 ♐ · 31 ♑	1 ♏	1 ♐ · 1 ♑ · 25 ♒	1 ♏ · 21 ♐	1 ♑ · 7 ♒	1 ♐ · 15 ♑	1 ♎ · 9 ♏	1 ♑ · 11 ♒

Zodiac sign key used below: ♈ Aries, ♉ Taurus, ♊ Gemini, ♋ Cancer, ♌ Leo, ♍ Virgo, ♎ Libra, ♏ Scorpio, ♐ Sagittarius, ♑ Capricorn, ♒ Aquarius, ♓ Pisces.

♀	1953	1954	1955	1956	1957	1958	1959	1960
JAN	1♒ 6♓	1♑ 23♒	1♏ 7♐	1♒ 8♓	1♐ 13♑	1♒	1♑ 8♒	1♏ 3♐ 28♑
FEB	1♓ 3♈	1♒ 16♓	1♐ 7♑	1♓ 12♈	1♑ 6♒	1♒	1♓ 25♈	1♑ 21♒
MAR	1♈ 15♉	1♓ ♈	1♑ ♒ ♓	1♈	1♒ 2♓ 26♈	1♒	1♈ 21♉	1♒ 16♓
APR	1♈	1♈ 5♉ 29♊	1♓ 25♈	1♈ 25♉	1♉ 19♊	1♒ 7♓	1♉ 15♊	1♓ 10♈
MAY	1♈	1♊ 24♋	1♈ 20♉	1♉ 20♊	1♊ 14♋	1♓ 6♈	1♊ 11♋	1♈ 4♉ 29♊
JUN	1♈ 6♉	1♋ 18♌	1♉ 14♊	1♊ 24♋	1♋ 7♊	1♈ 2♉ 27♊	1♋ 7♌	1♊ 22♋
JUL	1♉ 8♊	1♌ 14♍	1♊ 9♋	1♊	1♋ 2♌ 27♍	1♊ 22♋	1♌ 9♍	1♋ 16♌
AUG	1♊ 5♋ 31♌	1♍ 10♎	1♋ 2♌ 26♍	1♊ 5♋	1♍ 21♎	1♋ 16♌	1♍	1♌ 9♍
SEP	1♌ 25♍	1♎ 7♏	1♍ 19♎	1♋ 9♌	1♌ 15♍	1♌ 10♍	1♍ 21♎ 26♏	1♍ 3♎ 28♏
OCT	1♍ 18♎	1♏ 24♐ 28♏	1♎ 13♏	1♌ 7♍	1♍ 11♎	1♍ 3♎ 28♍	1♍	1♎ 22♏
NOV	1♎ 12♏	1♏	1♏ 6♐	1♍ 26♎	1♎ 6♏	1♏ 21♐	1♎ 10♏	1♏ 16♐
DEC	1♏ 6♐ 30♑	1♏	1♐ 25♑	1♎ 20♏	1♏ 7♐	1♐ 15♑	1♎ 8♏	1♏ 11♐

♀	1961	1962	1963	1964	1965	1966	1967	1968
JAN	1♒ 6♓	1♑ 22♒	1♏ 7♐	1♒ 17♓	1♐ 13♑	1♒	1♑ 7♒ 31♓	1♏ 2♐ 27♑
FEB	1♓ 3♈	1♒ 15♓	1♐ 6♑	1♓ 11♈	1♑ 6♒	1♒ 7♑ 26♒	1♓ 24♈	1♑ 21♒
MAR	1♈	1♓ ♈	1♑ 5♒ 31♓	1♈ 8♉	1♒ 2♓ 26♈	1♒	1♈ 21♉	1♒ 16♓
APR	1♈	1♈ 4♉ 29♊	1♓ 25♈	1♉ 5♊	1♉ 19♊	1♒ 7♓	1♉ 15♊	1♓ 9♈
MAY	1♈	1♊ 24♋	1♈ 19♉	1♊ 10♋	1♉ 13♊	1♈ 6♉	1♊ 11♋	1♈ 4♉ 28♊
JUN	1♈ 6♉	1♋ 18♌	1♉ 13♊	1♋ 18♊	1♋ 7♊	1♉ 27♊	1♊ 7♋	1♊ 21♋
JUL	1♉ 8♊	1♌ 13♍	1♊ 8♋	1♊	1♋ 26♌	1♊ 22♋	1♌ 9♍	1♋ 16♌
AUG	1♊ 4♋ 30♌	1♍ 8♎	1♊ 26♋	1♊ 6♋	1♌ 20♍	1♋ 16♌	1♍	1♌ 9♍
SEP	1♌ 24♍	1♎ 8♏	1♍ 18♎	1♋ 9♌	1♍ 14♎	1♌ 9♍	1♍ 10♎	1♍ 3♎ 27♏
OCT	1♍ 18♎	1♏	1♎ 13♏	1♌ 6♍	1♎ 10♏	1♍ 3♎ 27♏	1♌ 27♍	1♏ 22♐
NOV	1♎ 12♏	1♏	1♏ 6♐ 30♑	1♍ 25♎	1♏ 6♐	1♏ 20♐	1♎ 10♏	1♐ 15♑
DEC	1♏ 6♐ 29♑	1♏	1♑ 24♒	1♏ 20♐	1♐ 8♑	1♑ 22♒	1♎ 14♏	1♑ 10♒

– VENUS TABLES –

♀	1969	1970	1971	1972	1973	1974	1975	1976
JAN	1 ♒ 5 ♓	1 ♑ 22 ♒	1 ♏ 8 ♐	1 ♒ 17 ♓	1 ♐ 12 ♑	1 ♒ 30 ♑	1 ♑ 7 ♒ 31 ♓	1 ♏ 2 ♐ 27 ♑
FEB	1 ♓ 3 ♈	1 ♒ 15 ♓	1 ♐ 6 ♑	1 ♓ 11 ♈	1 ♑ 5 ♒	1 ♑	1 ♓ 24 ♈	1 ♑ 20 ♒
MAR	1 ♈	1 ♓ 11 ♈	1 ♑ 5 ♒ 30 ♓	1 ♈ 8 ♉	1 ♓ 25 ♈	1 ♒	1 ♈ 20 ♉	1 ♒ 15 ♓
APR	1 ♈	1 ♈ 4 ♉ 28 ♊	1 ♓ 24 ♈	1 ♉ 4 ♊	1 ♈ 19 ♉	1 ♒ 7 ♓	1 ♉ 14 ♊	1 ♓ 9 ♈
MAY	1 ♈	1 ♊ 23 ♋	1 ♈ 19 ♉	1 ♊	1 ♉ 13 ♊	1 ♓ 5 ♈	1 ♊ 10 ♋	1 ♈ 3 ♉ 27 ♊
JUN	1 ♈ 6 ♉	1 ♋ 17 ♌	1 ♉ 13 ♊	1 ♊	1 ♊ 6 ♋	1 ♉ 26 ♊	1 ♋ 7 ♌	1 ♊ 21 ♋
JUL	1 ♉ 7 ♊	1 ♌ 13 ♍	1 ♊ 7 ♋	1 ♊	1 ♌ 26 ♍	1 ♊ 22 ♋	1 ♌ 10 ♍	1 ♋ 15 ♌
AUG	1 ♊ 4 ♋ 30 ♌	1 ♍ 25 ♎	1 ♌ 25 ♍	1 ♊ 7 ♋	1 ♍ 19 ♎	1 ♋ 15 ♌	1 ♍	1 ♌ 9 ♍
SEP	1 ♌ 24 ♍	1 ♎ 8 ♏	1 ♍ 18 ♎	1 ♋ 8 ♌	1 ♎ 14 ♏	1 ♌ 9 ♍	1 ♍ 3 ♌	1 ♍ 2 ♎ 26 ♏
OCT	1 ♍ 18 ♎	1 ♏	1 ♍ 12 ♎	1 ♌ 6 ♍ 31 ♎	1 ♏ 9 ♐	1 ♍ 3 ♎ 27 ♏	1 ♌ 5 ♍	1 ♏ 21 ♐
NOV	1 ♎ 11 ♏	1 ♏	1 ♏ 5 ♐ 30 ♑	1 ♎ 25 ♏	1 ♐ 6 ♑	1 ♏ 20 ♐	1 ♍ 10 ♎	1 ♐ 15 ♑
DEC	1 ♏ 5 ♐ 29 ♑	1 ♏	1 ♑ 24 ♒	1 ♏ 19 ♐	1 ♑ 8 ♒	1 ♐ 14 ♑	1 ♎ 7 ♏	1 ♑ 10 ♒

♀	1977	1978	1979	1980	1981	1982	1983	1984
JAN	1 ♒ 5 ♓	1 ♑ 21 ♒	1 ♏ 8 ♐	1 ♒ 16 ♓	1 ♐ 12 ♑	1 ♒ 24 ♑	1 ♑ 6 ♒ 30 ♓	1 ♏ 2 ♐ 26 ♑
FEB	1 ♓ 3 ♈	1 ♒ 14 ♓	1 ♐ 6 ♑	1 ♓ 10 ♈	1 ♑ 5 ♒ 28 ♓	1 ♑	1 ♓ 23 ♈	1 ♑ 20 ♒
MAR	1 ♈	1 ♓ 9 ♈	1 ♑ 4 ♒ 29 ♓	1 ♈ 7 ♉	1 ♓ 25 ♈	1 ♒	1 ♈ 20 ♉	1 ♒ 15 ♓
APR	1 ♈	1 ♈ 3 ♉ 28 ♊	1 ♓ 23 ♈	1 ♉ 4 ♊	1 ♈ 18 ♉	1 ♒ 7 ♓	1 ♉ 14 ♊	1 ♓ 8 ♈
MAY	1 ♈	1 ♊ 22 ♋	1 ♈ 18 ♉	1 ♊	1 ♉ 12 ♊	1 ♓ 5 ♈	1 ♊ 10 ♋	1 ♈ 3 ♉ 27 ♊
JUN	1 ♈ 7 ♉	1 ♋ 17 ♌	1 ♉ 12 ♊	1 ♊	1 ♊ 6 ♋	1 ♉ 26 ♊	1 ♋ 7 ♌	1 ♊ 21 ♋
JUL	1 ♉ 7 ♊	1 ♌ 12 ♍	1 ♊ 7 ♋ 31 ♌	1 ♊	1 ♌ 25 ♍	1 ♊ 21 ♋	1 ♌ 11 ♍	1 ♋ 15 ♌
AUG	1 ♊ 3 ♋ 29 ♌	1 ♍ 25 ♎	1 ♌ 25 ♍	1 ♊ 7 ♋	1 ♍ 19 ♎	1 ♋ 15 ♌	1 ♍ 28 ♌	1 ♌ 8 ♍
SEP	1 ♌ 23 ♍	1 ♎ 8 ♏	1 ♍ 18 ♎	1 ♋ 8 ♌	1 ♎ 13 ♏	1 ♌ 8 ♍	1 ♌	1 ♍ 2 ♎ 26 ♏
OCT	1 ♍ 17 ♎	1 ♏	1 ♎ 12 ♏	1 ♌ 5 ♍ 31 ♎	1 ♏ 6 ♐	1 ♍ 2 ♎ 26 ♏	1 ♌ 6 ♍	1 ♏ 21 ♐
NOV	1 ♎ 11 ♏	1 ♏	1 ♏ 5 ♐ 29 ♑	1 ♎ 25 ♏	1 ♐ 6 ♑	1 ♏ 19 ♐	1 ♍ 10 ♎	1 ♐ 14 ♑
DEC	1 ♏ 4 ♐ 28 ♑	1 ♏	1 ♑ 23 ♒	1 ♏ 19 ♐	1 ♑ 9 ♒	1 ♐ 12 ♑	1 ♎ 7 ♏	1 ♑ 10 ♒

♀	1985	1986	1987	1988	1989	1990	1991	1992
JAN	1 ♒ 5 ♓	1 ♑ 21 ♒	1 ♏ 8 ♐	1 ♏ 16 ♐	1 ♐ 11 ♑	1 ♒ 17 ♑	1 ♑ 6 ♒ 30 ♓	1 ♐ 26 ♑
FEB	1 ♓ 3 ♈	1 ♒ 14 ♓	1 ♐ 6 ♑	1 ♐ 10 ♑	1 ♑ 4 ♒ 28 ♓	1 ♑	1 ♓ 23 ♈	1 ♑ 19 ♒
MAR	1 ♈	1 ♓ 9 ♈	1 ♑ 24 ♒	1 ♈ 7 ♓	1 ♑ 24 ♈	1 ♑ 24 ♒	1 ♈	1 ♒ 14 ♓
APR	1 ♈	1 ♈ 3 ♉ 27 ♊	1 ♑ 23 ♓	1 ♉ 4 ♊	1 ♈ 17 ♉	1 ♈ 7 ♓	1 ♉ 13 ♊	1 ♓ 7 ♈
MAY	1 ♈	1 ♊ 22 ♋	1 ♈ 18 ♉	1 ♊ 18 ♋ 27 ♊	1 ♊ 12 ♋	1 ♈ 4 ♓ 31 ♈	1 ♊ 9 ♋	1 ♈ 2 ♉ 26 ♊
JUN	1 ♈ 7 ♉	1 ♋ 16 ♌	1 ♉ 12 ♊	1 ♊	1 ♋ 5 ♊ 30 ♌	1 ♉ 25 ♊	1 ♋ 7 ♌	1 ♊ 20 ♋
JUL	1 ♉ 7 ♊	1 ♌ 12 ♍	1 ♊ 6 ♋ 31 ♌	1 ♊	1 ♌ 24 ♍	1 ♊ 20 ♋	1 ♌ 11 ♍	1 ♋ 14 ♌
AUG	1 ♊ 3 ♋ 28 ♌	1 ♍ 8 ♎	1 ♌ 24 ♍	1 ♊ 24 ♋	1 ♍ 18 ♎	1 ♋ 13 ♌	1 ♍ 22 ♎	1 ♌ 7 ♍
SEP	1 ♌ 23 ♍	1 ♎ 8 ♏	1 ♍ 17 ♎	1 ♋ 8 ♌	1 ♎ 13 ♏	1 ♌ 9 ♍	1 ♌	1 ♍ 25 ♎
OCT	1 ♍ 12 ♎	1 ♏	1 ♎ 11 ♏	1 ♌ 5 ♍ 30 ♎	1 ♏ 9 ♐	1 ♍ 2 ♎ 26 ♏	1 ♌ 7 ♍	1 ♏ 20 ♐
NOV	1 ♎ 10 ♏	1 ♏	1 ♏ 4 ♐ 28 ♑	1 ♎ 24 ♏	1 ♐ 6 ♑	1 ♏ 19 ♐	1 ♍ 9 ♎	1 ♐ 14 ♑
DEC	1 ♏ 4 ♐ 28 ♑	1 ♏	1 ♑ 23 ♒	1 ♏ 18 ♐	1 ♑ 10 ♒	1 ♐ 13 ♑	1 ♎ 7 ♏	1 ♑ 9 ♒

♀	1993	1994	1995	1996	1997	1998	1999	2000
JAN	1 ♒ 4 ♓	1 ♑ 20 ♒	1 ♏ 8 ♐	1 ♏ 15 ♐	1 ♐ 10 ♑	1 ♑ 10 ♒	1 ♑ 5 ♒ 29 ♓	1 ♐ 25 ♑
FEB	1 ♓ 3 ♈	1 ♒ 13 ♓	1 ♐ 5 ♑	1 ♐ 9 ♑	1 ♑ 4 ♒ 28 ♓	1 ♑	1 ♓ 22 ♈	1 ♑ 19 ♒
MAR	1 ♈	1 ♓ 9 ♈	1 ♑ 3 ♒ 29 ♓	1 ♈ 6 ♓	1 ♑ 24 ♈	1 ♑ 24 ♒	1 ♈	1 ♒ 14 ♓
APR	1 ♈	1 ♈ 2 ♉ 27 ♊	1 ♓ 3 ♈	1 ♉ 4 ♊	1 ♈ 17 ♉	1 ♈ 7 ♓	1 ♉ 13 ♊	1 ♓ 7 ♈
MAY	1 ♈	1 ♊ 21 ♋	1 ♈ 17 ♉	1 ♊ 18 ♋	1 ♊	1 ♈ 4 ♓ 30 ♈	1 ♊ 9 ♋	1 ♈ 2 ♉ 26 ♊
JUN	1 ♈ 7 ♉	1 ♋ 15 ♌	1 ♉ 11 ♊	1 ♊	1 ♋ 4 ♊ 29 ♌	1 ♉ 25 ♊	1 ♋ 6 ♌	1 ♊ 19 ♋
JUL	1 ♉ 6 ♊	1 ♌ 12 ♍	1 ♊ 6 ♋ 30 ♌	1 ♊	1 ♌ 24 ♍	1 ♊ 20 ♋	1 ♌ 13 ♍	1 ♋ 14 ♌
AUG	1 ♊ 2 ♋ 28 ♌	1 ♍ 8 ♎	1 ♌ 23 ♍	1 ♊ 8 ♋	1 ♍ 18 ♎	1 ♋ 14 ♌	1 ♍ 16 ♎	1 ♌ 7 ♍
SEP	1 ♌ 22 ♍	1 ♎ 8 ♏	1 ♍ 17 ♎	1 ♋ 8 ♌	1 ♎ 12 ♏	1 ♌ 7 ♍	1 ♌	1 ♍ 25 ♎
OCT	1 ♍ 16 ♎	1 ♏	1 ♎ 11 ♏	1 ♌ 5 ♍ 30 ♎	1 ♏ 9 ♐	1 ♍ 2 ♎ 25 ♏	1 ♌ 8 ♍	1 ♏ 20 ♐
NOV	1 ♎ 9 ♏	1 ♏	1 ♏ 4 ♐ 28 ♑	1 ♎ 23 ♏	1 ♐ 6 ♑	1 ♏ 18 ♐	1 ♍ 10 ♎	1 ♐ 13 ♑
DEC	1 ♏ 3 ♐ 27 ♑	1 ♏	1 ♑ 22 ♒	1 ♏ 17 ♐	1 ♑ 12 ♒	1 ♐ 12 ♑	1 ♎ 6 ♏	1 ♑ 9 ♒

♂	1921	1922	1923	1924	1925	1926	1927	1928	1929	1930
JAN	1 ♒ · 5 ♓	1 ♏	1 ♓ · 21 ♈	1 ♏ · 19 ♐	1 ♈	1 ♐	1 ♉	1 ♐ · 19 ♑	1 ♊	1 ♑
FEB	1 ♓ · 13 ♈	1 ♏ · 18 ♐	1 ♈	1 ♐	1 ♈ · 5 ♉	1 ♐ · 9 ♑	1 ♉ · 22 ♊	1 ♑ · 28 ♒	1 ♊	1 ♑ · 6 ♒
MAR	1 ♈ · 25 ♉	1 ♐	1 ♈ · 4 ♉	1 ♐ · 6 ♑	1 ♉ · 24 ♊	1 ♑ · 23 ♒	1 ♊	1 ♒	1 ♊ · 10 ♋	1 ♒ · 17 ♓
APR	1 ♉	1 ♐	1 ♉ · 16 ♊	1 ♑ · 24 ♒	1 ♊	1 ♒	1 ♊ · 17 ♋	1 ♒ · 7 ♓	1 ♋	1 ♓ · 24 ♈
MAY	1 ♉ · 6 ♊	1 ♐	1 ♊ · 30 ♋	1 ♒	1 ♊ · 9 ♋	1 ♒ · 3 ♓	1 ♋	1 ♓ · 16 ♈	1 ♋ · 13 ♌	1 ♈
JUN	1 ♊ · 18 ♋	1 ♐	1 ♋	1 ♒ · 24 ♓	1 ♋ · 26 ♌	1 ♓ · 15 ♈	1 ♋ · 6 ♌	1 ♈ · 26 ♉	1 ♌	1 ♈ · 3 ♉
JUL	1 ♋	1 ♐	1 ♋ · 16 ♌	1 ♓	1 ♌	1 ♈	1 ♌ · 25 ♍	1 ♉	1 ♌ · 4 ♍	1 ♉ · 14 ♊
AUG	1 ♋ · 3 ♌	1 ♐	1 ♌ · 24 ♍	1 ♓ · 12 ♒	1 ♌ · 12 ♍	1 ♉	1 ♍	1 ♉ · 9 ♊	1 ♍ · 21 ♎	1 ♊ · 28 ♋
SEP	1 ♌ · 19 ♍	1 ♐ · 13 ♑	1 ♍	1 ♒	1 ♍ · 28 ♎	1 ♉	1 ♍ · 10 ♎	1 ♊ · 21 ♋	1 ♎	1 ♋
OCT	1 ♍	1 ♑ · 30 ♒	1 ♍ · 18 ♎	1 ♒ · 19 ♓	1 ♎	1 ♉	1 ♎ · 26 ♏	1 ♋	1 ♎ · 6 ♏	1 ♋ · 20 ♌
NOV	1 ♍ · 6 ♎	1 ♒	1 ♎	1 ♓	1 ♎ · 13 ♏	1 ♉	1 ♏	1 ♋	1 ♏ · 18 ♐	1 ♌
DEC	1 ♎ · 26 ♏	1 ♒ · 11 ♓	1 ♎ · 4 ♏	1 ♓ · 19 ♈	1 ♏ · 28 ♐	1 ♉	1 ♏ · 8 ♐	1 ♋ · 20 ♊	1 ♐ · 29 ♑	1 ♌

♂	1931	1932	1933	1934	1935	1936	1937	1938	1939	1940
JAN	1 ♌	1 ♑ · 18 ♒	1 ♍	1 ♒	1 ♎	1 ♒ · 14 ♓	1 ♎ · 5 ♏	1 ♓ · 30 ♈	1 ♏ · 29 ♐	1 ♓ · 4 ♈
FEB	1 ♌ · 16 ♋	1 ♒ · 25 ♓	1 ♍	1 ♒ · 4 ♓	1 ♎	1 ♓ · 22 ♈	1 ♏	1 ♈	1 ♐	1 ♈ · 17 ♉
MAR	1 ♋ · 30 ♌	1 ♓	1 ♍	1 ♓ · 14 ♈	1 ♎	1 ♈	1 ♏ · 13 ♐	1 ♈ · 12 ♉	1 ♐ · 21 ♑	1 ♉
APR	1 ♌	1 ♓ · 3 ♈	1 ♍	1 ♈ · 22 ♉	1 ♎	1 ♉	1 ♐	1 ♉ · 23 ♊	1 ♑	1 ♊
MAY	1 ♌	1 ♈ · 12 ♉	1 ♍	1 ♉	1 ♎	1 ♉ · 13 ♊	1 ♐ · 14 ♏	1 ♊	1 ♑ · 25 ♒	1 ♊ · 17 ♋
JUN	1 ♌ · 10 ♍	1 ♉ · 22 ♊	1 ♍	1 ♉ · 2 ♊	1 ♎	1 ♊ · 25 ♋	1 ♏	1 ♊ · 7 ♋	1 ♒	1 ♋
JUL	1 ♍ · 27 ♎	1 ♊	1 ♍ · 6 ♎	1 ♊ · 15 ♋	1 ♎ · 29 ♏	1 ♋	1 ♏	1 ♋ · 22 ♌	1 ♒ · 21 ♑	1 ♋ · 3 ♌
AUG	1 ♎	1 ♊ · 4 ♋	1 ♎ · 26 ♏	1 ♋ · 30 ♌	1 ♏	1 ♋ · 10 ♌	1 ♏ · 8 ♐	1 ♌	1 ♑	1 ♌ · 19 ♍
SEP	1 ♎ · 17 ♏	1 ♋ · 20 ♌	1 ♏	1 ♌	1 ♏ · 16 ♐	1 ♌ · 26 ♍	1 ♐ · 30 ♑	1 ♌ · 7 ♍	1 ♑ · 24 ♒	1 ♍
OCT	1 ♏ · 30 ♐	1 ♌	1 ♏ · 9 ♐	1 ♌ · 18 ♍	1 ♐ · 28 ♑	1 ♍	1 ♑	1 ♍ · 25 ♎	1 ♒	1 ♍ · 5 ♎
NOV	1 ♐	1 ♌ · 13 ♍	1 ♐ · 19 ♑	1 ♍	1 ♑	1 ♍ · 14 ♎	1 ♑ · 11 ♒	1 ♎	1 ♒ · 19 ♓	1 ♎ · 20 ♏
DEC	1 ♐ · 10 ♑	1 ♍	1 ♑ · 28 ♒	1 ♍ · 11 ♎	1 ♑ · 7 ♒	1 ♎	1 ♒ · 21 ♓	1 ♎ · 11 ♏	1 ♓	1 ♏

– MARS TABLES –

♂	1941	1942	1943	1944	1945	1946	1947	1948	1949	1950
JAN	1 ♏ 4 ♐	1 ♈ 11 ♉	1 ♐ 26 ♑	1 ♊	1 ♐ 5 ♑	1 ♋	1 ♑ 25 ♒	1 ♍	1 ♑ 4 ♒	1 ♎
FEB	1 ♐ 17 ♑	1 ♉	1 ♑	1 ♊	1 ♑ 14 ♒	1 ♋	1 ♒	1 ♍ 12 ♌	1 ♒ 11 ♓	1 ♎
MAR	1 ♑	1 ♉ 7 ♊	1 ♑ 8 ♒	1 ♊ 29 ♋	1 ♒ 25 ♓	1 ♋	1 ♒ 4 ♓	1 ♌	1 ♓ 21 ♈	1 ♎ 28 ♍
APR	1 ♑ 2 ♒	1 ♊ 26 ♋	1 ♒ 17 ♓	1 ♋	1 ♓	1 ♋ 22 ♌	1 ♓ 11 ♈	1 ♌	1 ♈ 30 ♉	1 ♍
MAY	1 ♒ 16 ♓	1 ♋	1 ♓ 27 ♈	1 ♋ 22 ♌	1 ♓ 3 ♈	1 ♌	1 ♈ 21 ♉	1 ♌ 18 ♍	1 ♉	1 ♍
JUN	1 ♓	1 ♋ 14 ♌	1 ♈	1 ♌	1 ♈ 11 ♉	1 ♌ 20 ♍	1 ♉	1 ♍	1 ♉ 10 ♊	1 ♍ 11 ♎
JUL	1 ♓ 2 ♈	1 ♌	1 ♈ 7 ♉	1 ♌ 12 ♍	1 ♉ 23 ♊	1 ♍	1 ♊	1 ♍ 17 ♎	1 ♊ 23 ♋	1 ♎
AUG	1 ♈	1 ♍	1 ♉ 23 ♊	1 ♍ 29 ♎	1 ♊	1 ♍ 9 ♎	1 ♊ 13 ♋	1 ♎	1 ♋	1 ♎ 10 ♏
SEP	1 ♈	1 ♍ 17 ♎	1 ♊	1 ♎	1 ♊ 7 ♋	1 ♎ 24 ♏	1 ♋	1 ♎ 3 ♏	1 ♋ 7 ♌	1 ♏ 25 ♐
OCT	1 ♈	1 ♎	1 ♊	1 ♎ 13 ♏	1 ♋	1 ♏	1 ♌	1 ♏ 17 ♐	1 ♌ 27 ♍	1 ♐
NOV	1 ♈	1 ♎ 2 ♏	1 ♊	1 ♏ 25 ♐	1 ♋ 11 ♌	1 ♏ 6 ♐	1 ♌	1 ♐ 26 ♑	1 ♍	1 ♐ 6 ♑
DEC	1 ♈	1 ♏ 15 ♐	1 ♊	1 ♐	1 ♌ 26 ♋	1 ♐ 17 ♑	1 ♍	1 ♑	1 ♍ 26 ♎	1 ♑ 15 ♒

♂	1951	1952	1953	1954	1955	1956	1957	1958	1959	1960
JAN	1 ♒ 22 ♓	1 ♎ 20 ♏	1 ♓	1 ♏	1 ♓ 15 ♈	1 ♏ 14 ♐	1 ♈ 28 ♉	1 ♐	1 ♉	1 ♐ 14 ♑
FEB	1 ♓	1 ♏	1 ♓ 8 ♈	1 ♏ 9 ♐	1 ♈ 26 ♉	1 ♐ 28 ♑	1 ♉	1 ♐ 3 ♑	1 ♉ 10 ♊	1 ♑ 23 ♒
MAR	1 ♓ 2 ♈	1 ♏	1 ♈ 20 ♉	1 ♐	1 ♉	1 ♑	1 ♉ 17 ♊	1 ♑ 17 ♒	1 ♊	1 ♒
APR	1 ♈ 10 ♉	1 ♏	1 ♉	1 ♐ 12 ♑	1 ♉ 10 ♊	1 ♑ 14 ♒	1 ♊	1 ♒ 27 ♓	1 ♊ 10 ♋	1 ♒ 2 ♓
MAY	1 ♉ 21 ♊	1 ♏	1 ♊	1 ♑	1 ♊ 26 ♋	1 ♒	1 ♊ 4 ♋	1 ♓	1 ♋	1 ♓ 11 ♈
JUN	1 ♊	1 ♏	1 ♊ 14 ♋	1 ♑	1 ♋	1 ♒ 3 ♓	1 ♋ 21 ♌	1 ♓ 7 ♈	1 ♋ 2 ♌	1 ♈ 20 ♉
JUL	1 ♊ 3 ♋	1 ♏	1 ♋ 29 ♌	1 ♑	1 ♋ 11 ♌	1 ♓	1 ♌	1 ♈ 21 ♉	1 ♌ 20 ♍	1 ♉
AUG	1 ♋ 18 ♌	1 ♏ 27 ♐	1 ♌	1 ♑	1 ♌ 27 ♍	1 ♓	1 ♌ 8 ♍	1 ♉	1 ♍	1 ♉ 2 ♊
SEP	1 ♌	1 ♐	1 ♌ 14 ♍	1 ♑	1 ♍	1 ♓	1 ♍ 24 ♎	1 ♉ 21 ♊	1 ♍ 5 ♎	1 ♊ 21 ♋
OCT	1 ♌ 5 ♍	1 ♐ 12 ♑	1 ♍	1 ♑ 21 ♒	1 ♍ 13 ♎	1 ♓	1 ♎	1 ♊ 28 ♉	1 ♎ 21 ♏	1 ♋
NOV	1 ♍ 24 ♎	1 ♑ 21 ♒	1 ♎	1 ♒	1 ♎ 29 ♏	1 ♓	1 ♎ 8 ♏	1 ♉	1 ♏	1 ♋
DEC	1 ♎	1 ♒ 30 ♓	1 ♎ 20 ♏	1 ♒ 4 ♓	1 ♏	1 ♓ 6 ♈	1 ♏ 23 ♐	1 ♉	1 ♏ 3 ♐	1 ♋

♂	1961	1962	1963	1964	1965	1966	1967	1968	1969	1970
JAN	1♋	1♑	1♌	1♑ 13♒	1♍	1♒ 30♓	1♎	1♒ 9♓	1♏	1♓ 24♈
FEB	1♋ 5♊ 7♋	1♑ 2♒	1♌	1♒ 20♓	1♍	1♓	1♎ 12♏	1♓ 17♈	1♏ 25♐	1♈
MAR	1♋	1♒ 12♓	1♌	1♓ 29♈	1♍	1♓ 9♈	1♏ 31♎	1♈ 27♉	1♐	1♈ 7♉
APR	1♋	1♓ 19♈	1♌	1♈	1♍	1♈ 17♉	1♎	1♉	1♐	1♉ 18♊
MAY	1♋ 6♌	1♈ 28♉	1♌	1♈ 7♉	1♍	1♉ 28♊	1♎	1♉ 8♊	1♐	1♊
JUN	1♌ 28♍	1♉	1♌ 3♍	1♉ 17♊	1♍ 29♎	1♊	1♎	1♊ 21♋	1♐	1♊ 2♋
JUL	1♍	1♉ 9♊	1♍ 27♎	1♊ 30♋	1♎	1♊ 11♋	1♎ 19♏	1♋	1♐	1♋ 18♌
AUG	1♍ 17♎	1♊ 22♋	1♎	1♋	1♎ 20♏	1♋ 25♌	1♏	1♋ 5♌	1♐	1♌
SEP	1♎	1♋	1♎ 12♏	1♋ 15♌	1♏	1♌	1♏ 10♐	1♌ 21♍	1♐ 21♑	1♌ 3♍
OCT	1♎ 2♏	1♋ 11♌	1♏ 25♐	1♌	1♏ 4♐	1♌ 12♍	1♐ 23♑	1♍	1♑	1♍ 20♎
NOV	1♏ 13♐	1♌	1♐	1♌ 6♍	1♐ 14♑	1♍	1♑	1♍ 9♎	1♑ 4♒	1♎
DEC	1♐ 24♑	1♌	1♐ 5♑	1♍	1♑ 23♒	1♍ 4♎	1♑ 2♒	1♎ 29♏	1♒ 15♓	1♎ 6♏

♂	1971	1972	1973	1974	1975	1976	1977	1978	1979	1980
JAN	1♏ 23♐	1♈	1♐	1♉	1♏ 21♐	1♊	1♑	1♌ 26♋	1♑ 20♒	1♍
FEB	1♐	1♈ 10♉	1♐ 12♑	1♉ 27♊	1♐	1♊	1♑ 9♒	1♋	1♒ 28♓	1♍
MAR	1♐ 12♑	1♉ 27♊	1♑ 27♒	1♊	1♐ 3♑	1♊ 18♋	1♒ 20♓	1♋	1♓	1♍ 12♎
APR	1♑	1♊	1♒	1♊ 20♋	1♑ 11♒	1♋	1♓ 28♈	1♋ 11♌	1♓ 7♈	1♎
MAY	1♑ 3♒	1♊ 12♋	1♒ 8♓	1♋	1♒ 21♓	1♋ 16♌	1♈	1♌	1♈ 16♉	1♎ 4♍
JUN	1♒	1♋ 28♌	1♓ 21♈	1♋ 9♌	1♓	1♌	1♈ 6♉	1♌ 14♍	1♉ 26♊	1♍
JUL	1♒	1♌	1♈	1♌ 27♍	1♈	1♌ 7♍	1♉ 18♊	1♍	1♊	1♍ 11♎
AUG	1♒	1♌ 15♍	1♈ 12♉	1♍	1♈ 14♉	1♍ 24♎	1♊	1♍ 4♎	1♊ 8♋	1♎ 29♏
SEP	1♒	1♍	1♉	1♍ 12♎	1♉	1♎	1♋	1♎ 20♏	1♋ 25♌	1♏
OCT	1♒	1♎	1♉ 30♈	1♎ 28♏	1♉ 17♊	1♎ 9♏	1♋ 27♌	1♏	1♌	1♏ 12♐
NOV	1♒ 6♓	1♎ 15♏	1♈	1♏	1♊	1♏ 21♐	1♌	1♏ 2♐	1♌ 20♍	1♐ 22♑
DEC	1♓ 26♈	1♏ 30♐	1♈ 24♉	1♏ 11♐	1♊	1♐	1♌	1♐ 13♑	1♍	1♑ 31♒

♂	1981	1982	1983	1984	1985	1986	1987	1988	1989	1990
JAN	1 ♒	1 ♌	1 ♒ 17 ♓	1 ♎ 11 ♏	1 ♓	1 ♏	1 ♓ 8 ♈	1 ♏ 9 ♐	1 ♈ 19 ♉	1 ♐ 30 ♑
FEB	1 ♒ 7 ♓	1 ♌	1 ♓ 25 ♈	1 ♏	1 ♓ 3 ♈	1 ♏ 2 ♐	1 ♈ 21 ♉	1 ♐ 22 ♑	1 ♉	1 ♑
MAR	1 ♓ 17 ♈	1 ♌	1 ♈	1 ♏	1 ♈ 15 ♉	1 ♐ 28 ♑	1 ♉	1 ♑	1 ♉ 11 ♊	1 ♑ 12 ♒
APR	1 ♈ 25 ♉	1 ♌	1 ♈ 5 ♉	1 ♏	1 ♉ 26 ♊	1 ♑	1 ♉ 6 ♊	1 ♑ 7 ♒	1 ♊ 29 ♋	1 ♒ 21 ♓
MAY	1 ♉	1 ♌	1 ♉ 17 ♊	1 ♏	1 ♊	1 ♑	1 ♊ 21 ♋	1 ♒ 22 ♓	1 ♋	1 ♓ 31 ♈
JUN	1 ♉ 5 ♊	1 ♌	1 ♊ 29 ♋	1 ♏	1 ♊ 9 ♋	1 ♑	1 ♋	1 ♓	1 ♋ 17 ♌	1 ♈
JUL	1 ♊ 18 ♋	1 ♌	1 ♋	1 ♏	1 ♋ 25 ♌	1 ♑	1 ♋ 7 ♌	1 ♓ 14 ♈	1 ♌	1 ♈ 13 ♉
AUG	1 ♋	1 ♌ 3 ♍	1 ♋ 14 ♌	1 ♏ 18 ♐	1 ♌	1 ♑	1 ♌ 23 ♍	1 ♈	1 ♌ 3 ♍	1 ♉ 31 ♊
SEP	1 ♋ 2 ♌	1 ♍ 20 ♐	1 ♌ 30 ♍	1 ♐	1 ♌ 10 ♍	1 ♑	1 ♍	1 ♈	1 ♍ 20 ♎	1 ♊
OCT	1 ♌ 21 ♍	1 ♐	1 ♍	1 ♐ 5 ♑	1 ♍ 28 ♎	1 ♑ 9 ♒	1 ♍ 9 ♎	1 ♈ 24 ♓	1 ♎	1 ♊
NOV	1 ♍	1 ♑	1 ♍ 18 ♎	1 ♑ 16 ♒	1 ♎	1 ♒ 26 ♓	1 ♎ 24 ♏	1 ♓ 2 ♈	1 ♎ 4 ♏	1 ♊
DEC	1 ♍ 16 ♎	1 ♑ 10 ♒	1 ♎	1 ♒ 25 ♓	1 ♎ 15 ♏	1 ♓	1 ♏	1 ♈	1 ♏ 18 ♐	1 ♊ 14 ♉

♂	1991	1992	1993	1994	1995	1996	1997	1998	1999	2000
JAN	1 ♉ 21 ♊	1 ♐ 9 ♑	1 ♋	1 ♑ 28 ♒	1 ♍ 23 ♌	1 ♑ 3 ♒	1 ♍ 3 ♎	1 ♒ 25 ♓	1 ♎ 26 ♏	1 ♒ 4 ♓
FEB	1 ♊	1 ♑ 18 ♒	1 ♋	1 ♒	1 ♌	1 ♒ 15 ♓	1 ♎	1 ♓	1 ♏	1 ♓ 12 ♈
MAR	1 ♊	1 ♒ 28 ♓	1 ♋	1 ♒ 7 ♓	1 ♌	1 ♓ 25 ♈	1 ♎ 9 ♍	1 ♓ 5 ♈	1 ♏	1 ♈ 23 ♉
APR	1 ♊ 3 ♋	1 ♓	1 ♋ 28 ♌	1 ♓ 15 ♈	1 ♌	1 ♈	1 ♍	1 ♈ 13 ♉	1 ♏	1 ♉
MAY	1 ♋ 27 ♌	1 ♓ 6 ♈	1 ♌	1 ♈ 24 ♉	1 ♌ 26 ♍	1 ♈ 3 ♉	1 ♍	1 ♉ 24 ♊	1 ♏ 6 ♎	1 ♉ 4 ♊
JUN	1 ♌	1 ♈ 15 ♉	1 ♌ 23 ♍	1 ♉	1 ♍	1 ♉ 12 ♊	1 ♍ 19 ♎	1 ♊	1 ♎	1 ♊ 16 ♋
JUL	1 ♌ 16 ♍	1 ♉ 27 ♊	1 ♍	1 ♉ 4 ♊	1 ♍ 21 ♎	1 ♊ 26 ♋	1 ♎	1 ♊ 6 ♋	1 ♎ 5 ♏	1 ♋
AUG	1 ♍	1 ♊	1 ♍ 12 ♎	1 ♊ 17 ♋	1 ♎	1 ♋	1 ♎ 14 ♏	1 ♋ 21 ♌	1 ♏	1 ♌
SEP	1 ♎	1 ♊ 12 ♋	1 ♎ 27 ♏	1 ♋	1 ♎ 7 ♏	1 ♋ 10 ♌	1 ♏ 29 ♐	1 ♌	1 ♏ 3 ♐	1 ♌ 17 ♍
OCT	1 ♎ 17 ♏	1 ♋	1 ♏	1 ♋ 5 ♌	1 ♏ 21 ♐	1 ♌ 30 ♍	1 ♐	1 ♌ 7 ♍	1 ♐ 17 ♑	1 ♍
NOV	1 ♏ 29 ♐	1 ♋	1 ♏ 9 ♐	1 ♌	1 ♐	1 ♍	1 ♐ 9 ♑	1 ♍ 27 ♎	1 ♑ 26 ♒	1 ♍ 4 ♎
DEC	1 ♐	1 ♋	1 ♐ 20 ♑	1 ♌ 12 ♍	1 ♑	1 ♍	1 ♑ 18 ♒	1 ♎	1 ♒	1 ♎ 23 ♏